John Calvin Rezmerski | *Cataloging the Flow: Elegy*

John Calvin Rezmerski

Cataloging the Flow: Elegy

Red Dragonfly Press

ISBN 978-1-945063-02-2

Cover photograph: "Cannon River near Red Wing"
by Scott King,

Designed and typeset by Scott King
using Dante MT Std

Published by Red Dragonfly Press
307 Oxford Street
Northfield, MN 55057
www.reddragonflypress.org

Cataloging the Flow: Elegy

"And for all this, nature is never spent"
—Gerard Manley Hopkins

I

Between threads of clouded current, granular windings
of shifting sand and tangled clumps of wet-stemmed
vegetation, unplotted stripings of black or tan—

Old bare banks become re-heaped midstream sandbars,
mudflats morph into resting-places:

for amphibians, for abandoned bikes forgotten by thieves,
for ancient weapons, and for occasional lost purses
ornamented with glowering thunderbirds' man-made grins.

Where once windmills and cabins were,
now antennas and polebarns shine.

Where once was corn, some mornings we see
skinny turkeys crossing meadows of goldenrod.

Once where great foundation rocks stuck up,
holes peppered with gravel now puddle.

Here a house, a barn, a shed, a silo once
painted white, now collapsing into gray.

Crumbs of glass are ground like chicken grit into
a rough yard where once children *liked* to peck
at each other like chickens *had* to.

Oxcart tracks once visible at the base of the bluff
now lie somewhere under brush, while in some yards
immigrant boxelders and hackberries have lost favor
to gingkos and Russian olives, but that can't last.

Twenty-five fathoms deep The River Warren ran here
ten thousand years ago, the anglers say,
while fishing the Minnesota's twisted trickle.

Big catfish lie low in places, and loads of trash fish,
but where have the bass and trout swum or bellied-up?

Bare banks become sandbars become mudflats
where trees lie down to sleep at last nearby turtles.

Once music once thumped once within the farmhouse,
and now crushed beer cans clutter its still heart
while the music passes by in cars.

Unaccounted for and unaccountable to anyone,
a long way from any house that it could fit,
a perfectly mortared brick chimney lies in a ditch.

Against a fence a solitary morning glory leans.

Bottles that used to offer Schiedam Schnapps
grind slowly into silica powder among the rocks.

Once attached to a buffalo, a chalky horn divorced from its skull
washes up and is assigned a place on a mahogany coffee table,
while a pair of maple coffee tables gets tossed
into a grove clustered with busted and rusted machines,
and come spring when the water's up
the tables wash away and the iron budges a bit.

A hornets' nest blown down and trod on barefoot
is one more pain driving a kid to the city.

When the world was all new, Unktehi the water demon
made the river overflow and scrub the hills bare.
But it was not he who leached the nitrates
and phosphates free into the fishy world.

Tin dishes, tiny Green Giants, feather ticking, coloring books—
landfills full of waste plain as Jesus on a pizza,
and sewage plants where lost wedding rings turn up,
and cemeteries planted not high enough above the flood
to keep undisturbed the remains of those who do not remain,
and ghost towns haunted by forgotten names,
and hospitals where fluids are extracted and infused,
and fields once full of flax to wear, that now bloom
with corn ethanol set to belch a hydrocarbon reek—

it all makes its way along this time-bound river,
swirling in eddies of entropy, highways and sidewalks
headed the way of the steel rivers of railroads gone missing
or sending tendrils to embrace obsolete power plants.

Remember this river is where boys drowned,
where frogs sported extra legs, mussels went missing,
and heavy metals learned to burden our fears.
Cattle now and then waded in too deep,
slipped down the slick and sucking banks
to get stuck in mud that made short work of them,
geologically speaking.

Remember when and where you were when
the climate went south, if you think you might
survive long enough for anyone to listen.

Shabby remains of a last-year's duck blind,
a shiny new machine shed dwarfing the trailer
where the owner is raising his hockey players,
beanfields spotted with volunteer corn
and rebellious pigweed, aluminum skeletons
and dead refrigerators, houses shedding shingles,
collapsing into their cellars with "Peace"
spray-painted on their crumbling walls,
beer being pissed onto the last coals of campfires,
empty packets of cigarettes crumpled in corners,
brands once available in stores now boarded up—

all where the river of weary manufacturing
dries up and becomes elbow lakes of refuse.

The River Warren settled to become the Minnesota,
the Minnesota of two hundred years ago,
became the Minnesota of settlement, sediment, sentiment—
a hundred years from now, who knows?

Before the River Warren, there was the inland sea,
Lake Agassiz, and where is it now?

Downstream,
downstream,
along with all the rain, dew, spit,
dumped-out coffee and sour milk
from all the ditches and feeder streams,

Chippewa, Yellow Medicine, Cottonwood,
Redwood, Maple, Blue Earth, Carver, Purgatory,
and all, not to mention municipal sewers,
downstream,
downstream.

II

Remember where and when you watched
the rowboat drift past, imagined a man and woman
stretched out engaged fully belly to belly—
unaware of anyone fishing in the shadow
of a fallen oak and watching the
rubbing and writhing—and heard them moan,
reminding us of another season already slid southward,
carrying along the voices of the Canada geese
engaged in the conversation nature demands—
first things first, then fish.

Tickles of homesick tears and aching
thoughts of days on the road
at last settled down around nighttime bonfires
on farms above the floodplain,
where involuntary pigs would sizzle and send
their savor through groves where
tinder could be gathered for cheery flames—

those were *some* parties: the beer and bratwurst,
volleyball, children full of beans,
parental salads, good or not so good, confections of gossip,
philosophy, sport, flirtations,
lines dropped into the river, drifting fishward,
driftwood gathered with dreams of carpentry,
nettles stinging legs along the path,
and old sweet songs and ribald riddles posed,
campfire smoke stinging eyes,
gentle chuckles at mild misfortune—
and not so many decades ago, we might suppose,
similar giggles in games of archery,
in gathering of tubers and berries, voices

bantering between in-laws and lodge-brothers
sharing savory meat and nettles boiled with hot rocks,
the games of who could bring in the most game—
at least till the buffalo were near gone—
the most rosehips, prairie turnips, getting ready
for winter pemmican and nourishing stories
in snow-dusted tipis in careful villages
in the old days of lore explored,
of older days and feral spirits that lured
the unwary into paths that go nowhere
and do not lead back where they came from,
and somehow wind toward the circles
where stories warn children of perils
of the hunt, and of the ways of strangers
out of the long past when great serpents
scoured the valley, and of strangers yet to come
covering the land with strange lodges,
scattering the woods with iron, scattering
the people away from homes and game—
till finally the deer were near gone—
bringing new rules of hunting, barrels
of pork not salted enough to keep from spoiling,
new diseases, smallpox, syphilis, homesickness,
new ways of treating the corpses of the dead.

In bark lodges and fifteen-poled tipis
and in the lately built frame shacks,
rattles communed with drums
and high-chest singing bewailed the dead,
honored heroes, and called the game—
until at last even the prairie chickens were gone.

Still, flutes in the night invited
head-to-head whispers hooded under blankets
conspiring to beget new generations
always, always, always, always.

The homes of the newcomers sometimes
overflowed with music, voices singing sometimes
different tunes at the same time.

Great chests of strings and hammers
on which to pound out the most delicate airs,
benches where two could sit side by side
pressing on gleaming ivories all in a row,
pumping up their spirits or meditating on
unvoiced sadnesses, or simply
being at play, competing with one another
to see who could tickle the most joy
out of just plain being together.

When they took possession of new homes,
they took along the strung wooden boxes
and discovered new tunes and recovered
joyful noise and somber rhythms and counterpoints,
visiting, resisting, and revisiting
the melodies they had made and craved,
and fed each other, and toasted their luck,
and eventually stopped playing,
hand and voices stilled by infirmity,
leaving families to hold heavy memories of
crescendos of brain and diminuendos of heart,
imagining glimpses of their departed musicians
riding down the spring floods on a spirit barge,

a barge shaped like a concert grand,
a red-haired Viking riding by the lid lifted
like a sail, or like a revival tent
sheltering a woman singing dark-haired hymns
whose words she once believed,
the two playing old music better than ever,
or improvising more music than they had learned,
while waving to their families
gathered on the banks,
while the river gushes and burbles out
its own tune.

Where did that barge of harmony go,
downstream,
downstream?
Has anybody seen it today, did it sink
or go drifting toward the holy ocean?
Or did we just dream that it goes on
downstream?

Skoal pa fisken!

Recall the once-upon-a-time gatherings on the sandbar
where the survivors now scatter the ashes,
remembering the musical days
of someone who did not make it this year,
except as these ashes graying the current, ashes
headed for parts known only as *somewhere*
a far piece down this river and the next,
the river's gurgles echoing suspicious hints
of "I'll take you home again, Kathleeen?"

Those memories are crests of longing,
and the dreams after all are just diversions
for us who cannot imagine our own deaths,
though now and again—
lying down or in a sudden silence—
we might perhaps maybe reluctantly imagine
our old companions singing us the goodbyes
that we have stood and sung ourselves, as prescribed
by long precedent, death by death.

We knew in private darkness
that breathing is now all up to us—
the living left behind: in. pause; out, pause;
in again—and out—the secret always to remember:
exhale the life-air, to carry some effluent
away from our hearts, air to which we have added
some feeling that might preserve words:

Ubi sunt qui ante nos fuerunt?
Where has the world gone
that once glowed for us
with such cooking—fire coals,
such neon, such krypton-charged vapor,
such fair blossoms, such fireworks in mimicry,
such moon or snows, salmon-stippled clouds at dusk,
such a river full of struggles to get upstream
where we might breed and fulfill the lives of bears,
our blood trickling, dissolving,
downstream,
downstream.

III

A languorous flow, the river, though:
discovery and work, memory and plans,
delight and disaster—transporter of homes,
on upriver barges, or washed downriver at flood-time—
deliverer of wildness, and even in parched seasons,
reminder of the essential wetness of life:
the river drinks what we drink,
slaked thirst anticipating flushed kidneys,
ooze of monthly blood and spurt of semen,
vessel of cooking broth, sluice
through which the salt of our gone bodies
is rinsed into the sea where newness is brewed
and waste is at last not wasted.
That we become compost sinking into earth
is not nature's revenge against us—
we are nature's revenge against indifference,
or at least its reply
to the hide-and-seek of slippery life and ready death.
I am it. *You* are it. To the river,
you, me, he, she, they, we,
are all mere *it*, a slight something
notable only for not being nothing.
Dead or alive is all one to the water.
That we solve problems of policy or engineering,
that we make love, or cry for hurt or loss
makes no matter for the river.
All the tears of all of us ever
have not swelled the current a micron—
the river is a great long tear itself,
insensible to trivial leakage of human sadness.

Nevertheless, weeping is elemental—
the river neither feels sympathy nor minds our grief—
caring is up to us.

If we are as bubbles and grains of sand in the current,
if we may become leather carbuncles in boxes under headstones,
along a river of songs and chants and rhymes and laughter
and prayers and readings and birdcalls and catcalls
and sweet something-nothings in each others' cars,
we will have joined the wind and the material rumor
that deserts, too, are variously beautiful—
However hot, however dry, however bare,
where something lived, something else may live again
given one seed, and some sun,
a little dew's a flood. Watch, wait.

Along the river this is how our hopes flow:

We are the knowledge of the link
between monarchs and milkweeds,
we are the fans the pelicans spread
in their great Shaker dance over riparian thermals.

Since the days of Raven's first flight,
century by century coming out on the earth
we have spoken our emergings and becomings:
Mound-builders, Pictograph-carvers, Dakota pipe-makers,
French traders, missionaries and Welsh and German settlers,
Scandinavian factions becoming a newly native Scandination.
Italians, Poles, Bohemians, Hmong refugees, Kisii students,
bringers of the varieties of Spanish, Arab, and Straits tongues—

Americans original, adopted, reconstructed, reborn,
world-hungry humans out for richer or for poorer
with traps and plows and hammers and cash-registers
on a taxing walk among the red willows and oaks,
big bluestem, soybeans, honeybees, grapes, and fireflies.
And corn. Yes, corn and its genetic surge of hundreds of names.
And the harvest, and the fall of leaves from umbrella to carpet.

We are the awareness of winter
burying all on the surface
while nursing spring down deep.

We are the creators of joy, anticipating
the sharp cracking of the ice
that scares the half-starved deer,
the disappearance of the coating of snow,
the bark of limb-tips swelling into buds.

Clots of fur, carcasses large and small,
ice-chewed bird wings, drowned dogs—
there is much in the way of winter-kill
to wash downstream,
making room for mating geese.

The deer have returned to trouble our gardens,
enchant our children and bother our bureaucracies—
and will and still will, despite our ammunition,
until they or other somethings, material or imaginary,
die too often and hunger itself becomes too hungry. . . .
Buffalo, too, are back, but bred for the butcher.
Customers plumbed with fat arteries

know more than they like to,
but live with it, conceding to ignorance
the details that do not augment flavor.

Insects, worms, serpents, molds, algae,
all awake to spring, but probably have not dreamed of it.

If not for us, who would appreciate
the tricks the wind plays on water?
Not the river, not the water-striders,
the pollywogs, the gusts and breezes themselves.

Peppermint was not peppermint until we tasted and named it.
Eagles mean nothing to fish but abrupt rips.
Earthquakes arouse no concern
among the chickadees and muskrats
about greater earthquakes yet to come.

Our old alliance with yeast was never properly ratified.
Health was only accidental until we noticed it,
drank it, gave it various labels and recipes.
All sentiment aside, all sediment settled,
we brewed beer both better and worse
than our ancestors ever had.

The butterfly medallions in treatment centers,
the bicycle trail where late the steel rails lay idle,
the apples and grapes at the university,
the asparagus in the ditches—that's our doing,
along with the beehives and bronze sculptures,
along with fiberglass pontoons, canoes, and PVC pipes,
and kissing at dusk, and blankets and stoves in winter hush,

and more stone blocks mounted on more stone blocks
to shelter those who live long enough.

Healthy appetites, hearty games, nutritious kisses,
soulful longings, regimens for popular varieties of sanity—
are we speeding toward happiness?
If it were not for us, time would have nowhere to go.

Bridges fall and threaten to fall and fall into disuse
and for all that, we build more and bigger.

In a few generations the stone age became the bronze age,
then the iron age and age of steel and concrete,
and eventually the age of plastic memory and tiny machines
that count dots, aughts, and oughts on imaginary fingers.

What age is next? An era of pure imagination at last?

Our works may not be solid enough,
may not live a moment longer than us—
but dying does not trump having lived.
In a no-trump universe, we are the tricks of evolution,
potential become possibility become posterity,
shifting banks of tributaries,
abstraction become an embrace—
we are the tick-tock of time playing tag
downstream,
downstream.

What can we make of ourselves being ourselves—
our fleeting efforts increments of creation?
Who will long remember what we note now or soon?

Ubi sunt qui post nos fuerunt?
Hundreds of years from now, thousands, sextillions,
somebody may know in every cell of the body
what kind of final river we have lived along,
how the universe may have been using us,
playing us, listing us, lifting us
downstream

ABOUT THE AUTHOR

John Calvin Rezmerski's works comprise twenty books, chapbooks, and anthologies, including *Breaking the Rules: Starting with Ghazals* and *Keeping Caedmon's Faith*, both by Red Dragonfly Press. His friend Carol Bly, the late author and social critic, said, "Rezmerski drags us past all the easy answers...toward the major passions." He has performed for hundreds of audiences—in theaters, schools, libraries, coffee houses, bars, museums, festivals, senior centers, and meetings of professional organizations, and on television and radio, including American Public Radio's *Whad'Ya Know?* He lives in Mankato, not far from the gathering waters of the Minnesota River.